Food Lessons in Love

Khanna Sutra

Dear Shan,

Happy Cooking.

Love

Vikas Khanna

First published in 2013

OM
Om Books International

Corporate & Editorial Office
A-12, Sector 64, Noida 201 301
Uttar Pradesh, India
Phone: +91 120 477 4100
Email: editorial@ombooks.com
Website: www.ombooksinternational.com

Sales Office
4379/4B, Prakash House, Ansari Road
Darya Ganj, New Delhi 110 002, India
Phone: +91 11 2326 3363, 2326 5303
Fax: +91 11 2327 8091
Email: sales@ombooks.com
Website: www.ombooks.com

Recipes copyright © Vikas Khanna
Photographs copyright © Vikas Khanna
Cover image: Michael Swamy
Design: Alpana Khare

ISBN: 978-93-81607-65-7

10 9 8 7 6 5 4 3 2 1

Printed in India

Food Lessons in Love

Khanna Sutra

Vikas Khanna

Foreword
Deepak Chopra

Om Books International

cont

ents

Foreword

When a chef has the simplicity of vision to step away from the expected and still be a part of an integrated cuisine, he is bound to generate interest in his food, beliefs and culture. Vikas Khanna is one such chef. His distinctive combination of ingredients and techniques creates dishes which reflect his passion for purity and a commitment to his roots.

Vikas is particualarly inclined towards his singular vision of sharing his heritage and the pursuit of excellence. I have reasons to believe that what is cooked by Vikas's hands is all a foundation of love for humanity. Having had his food at the restaurant, and served with the same integrity, he is an embodiment of Indian hospitality.

Khanna Sutra: Food Lessons in Love will help home cooks and professional chefs discover fresh and exciting ways of foraying into the whole institution of Indian cooking.

Deepak Chopra

All About Love

Love is life. All, everything that I understand,

I understand only because I love.

Everything is, everything exists, only because I love.

LEO TOLSTOY

There are many ways to look at the past – the discovery of the New Worlds, the rise and fall of empires, the lives of kings and queens or simply through the food and recipes passed down from one generation to another. Food has, since the beginning of time, done more than simply provide nourishment. It has been a powerful force in shaping civilisations, leading us through social transformation and laying the very foundation of the society we live in today.

Food is the essence of celebration. Any festival or ceremony is incomplete without a great feast, the experience of sharing it with one another, and of creating memories. And cooking a meal for somebody is an expression of utmost warmth and love, a reminder to people that they are special to us.

Months before February 14th, restaurants go into a frenzy to get ready for one of the busiest days of the year – the celebration of Valentine's Day. Every detail – from menus, to presentation, to execution – must be near flawless if we are to give the gift of the most perfect evening to our patrons and their loved ones.

Each year, our attempt is to get as creative as possible to bring to the table rich, decadent flavours, combining ingredients in ways that would add to the romantic experience.

The first time I heard Americans pronounce my name was when I landed in New York in the year 2000. To me it sounded like they said 'Khaan-na', which means food in Hindi. With all due respect to my family name, I must confess, I never ever corrected the American pronunciation because I was happy and even proud of this new approach to my last name, because food is my life.

Thus in February 2002, while drafting the menus for Salaam Bombay, my colleague Remya Warrier suggested we name the Valentine's Day Menu – 'Khanna Sutra'. Hence the name, the book and this dimension of food were born.

Over the last 10 years, I have been hosting and creating Valentine's Day menus and presenting them in new avatars. I take inspiration from a spice or ingredient which is believed to be aphrodisiac in nature, and weave a dish around that ingredient. In this book are the little lessons (*sutras*) that I learned in the recipe development of the menus. Here I bring to your kitchens *Khanna Sutra: Food Lessons in Love*, developed with passion, simplicity and pure regard for love.

The term 'aphrodisiac' is derived from the name of the Greek Goddess of Love – Aphrodite. Different cultures and civilisations, from the Romans to the Greeks, to the Chinese and even the Hindus had their own beliefs about what foods were aids to love and fertility. Usually a combination of the aroma, flavour, texture and appearance of certain ingredients earned them a place in history as aphrodisiacs.

Folklore has made a great contribution to the list of known aphrodisiacs. Apples – the forbidden fruit of the Garden of Eden, oysters – Goddess Aphrodite rose from the sea on an oyster shell and even spices were mentioned in *The Perfumed Garden* of the Arabs as well as the *Kama Sutra* as timeless catalysts of passion.

Passion is mysterious, elusive; it is desired but difficult to capture; we know it when we feel it but do not always know how to invoke it. We spend vast fortunes to make ourselves more appealing: perfumes, silks, make-up, scented candles, exotic luxury foods and drinks.

I recall one Valentine's Day. After a long and busy shift, on my way out of the restaurant, I happened to hear a customer on his cell phone, complaining loudly: 'I take this girl for Valentine's Dinner, I pay $200 and all she wants to know is who made the dessert!' Needless to say, I kept my head down and walked away as fast as I could from the angry gentleman. Later that night, on my way home in the subway, I began to realise the power of food to arouse emotions. That became the mantra and the foundation of this project.

Khanna Sutra is a book of recipes celebrating the tradition of sensuous eating.

There are many ingredients believed to promote passion but we will confine ourselves to the culinary ingredients that have wonderful scents, flavours and textures, and that also stimulate us visually. These recipes are not strictly Indian in the classical sense of traditional Indian cuisine but they are definitely Indian in terms of their orientation towards the country of my birth.

I have to say, while writing the recipes for *Khanna Sutra,* I did in fact have a great time. I gave myself the freedom to experiment, browsing through the aisles of stores, looking for inspiration, my objective being to create recipes that were both flavourful and beautiful. Combining these new finds with age-old ingredients was a thoroughly enjoyable challenge and I highly recommend that while cooking recipes from this book, do experiment; there is immense satisfaction in discovering that the chance you took on a flavour, turned out quite well, after all.

We have tried to focus on recipes that allow the special ingredients to stand out. The ingredients of passion vary from one culture to another and we have tried here to give each nation its due. If you find that we have left out some prized ingredient from your repertoire, write to us and we will include it in subsequent editions. We hope that you experience the same joy that we do when we serve these dishes to our loved ones.

Vikas Khanna

Aphrodisiacs

AlmondsApricotsArtichokes
AsafoetidaAsparagusAvocado
BeetrootCardamomCelery
CinnamonCucumberDates
ChilliPeppersChocolateCilantroCoriander
EggsFennelFenugreek
GarlicGojiBerriesHoney
MangoesMintMushroom
NutmegOystersPeaches
BlackPeppercornsPassionFruitPineNuts
PomegranateRoseRosemary
SaffronTomatoesVanillaYams

Almonds

In her infinite wisdom, nature has packaged all possible benefits in every element of the earth. One great gift of nature is almonds. Almonds are given as tokens of good fortune and happiness on auspicious occasions. It is believed that Samson courted Delilah with fragrant almonds. There also existed an old Roman tradition of showering almonds on newlyweds as a fertility rite. There are two types of almonds – sweet and bitter. The sweet variety, commonly used in recipes, adds a nutty fragrance and flavour and is a nutritious and healthy addition to any dish. Almonds can be bought shelled, with skin, or blanched without skin.

Apricots

In the symbolic powers of the flora kingdom, apricots are considered the symbol of love. According to Jacqueline M. Newman, in Chinese food symbolism, apricots stand for a beautiful woman. Apricots have been considered an aphrodisiac since their appearance in William Shakespeare's *A Midsummer Night's Dream*. Apricots come in many varieties – the colour of the skin ranges from pale yellow to deep orange and the flesh – a golden-cream colour to a brilliant orange. The skin is velvety, with a slight fuzz. The flesh is firm, sweet and delicately aromatic, but contains little juice. Used in Middle Eastern savoury dishes such as pilafs, apricots add a slight sweetness. They can be eaten raw or cooked and are available both fresh and dried. Apricots can be used to flavour both sweet and savoury dishes and add a delicate fruitiness when puréed into beverages.

Artichokes

Artichoke is a plant native to southern Europe, North Africa, and the Canary Islands. In the 16th century, it was considered an aphrodisiac and was reserved for men alone. At the core of the artichoke is its 'heart' – making the artichoke a symbol of love and hope for successful future relationships. In the *Book of Nature* by Dr Bartolomeo Boldo, published 1576 he says, 'It has the virtue of… provoking Venus for both men and women.' The best artichokes have dark green, heavy and tight leaves. The heart of the choke is edible, and is the favourite part of the artichoke for some. The leaves closest to the heart of the artichoke are the tenderest. Baby artichokes are fully mature artichokes that grow closer to the ground, sheltered by the larger leaves on the plant. They are easy to cook and prepare because the inner fuzzy portion of the artichoke remains undeveloped.

Asafoetida

Ayurveda is the science of natural healing in India. It considers asafoetida one of the most prized spices in the world. Asafoetida is a strongly fragrant, dried brownish resin extracted from the root of a plant found mainly in the wild from the eastern Mediterranean to Central Asia. It is available in two forms – in lumps or in powdered form. It is a mixture of resin and corn flour, often with salt and some colouring added too. It adds an intriguing bitter-sweet, slightly earthy tang, which lends richness and depth to many dishes and complements the flavours of many other Indian spices. Its fragrance and flavour become milder and pleasing to smell when heated in oil. It takes on the taste and aroma reminiscent of sautéed garlic. It is also used in Persian and Mediterranean cuisine. In India, it is used especially by the followers of Jainism and Vaishnavism who do not eat onions or garlic, in many vegetarian and lentil dishes to add both flavour and aroma. In southern India, asafoetida is used in their spice mixtures. It is used for seasoning only vegetables as vegetarianism is more common in southern India.

Asparagus

A vision of asparagus in one's dream signifies prosperous surroundings. In 19th-century France, bridegrooms were served three courses of these delicious spears at their prenuptial dinner. It received great attention in 17th-century French cookbooks. Asparagus-growing beds in northern Italy were famous during the Renaissance period. This delicate spring vegetable has always been a symbol of elegance and, in earlier times, was a delicacy only the wealthy could afford. In the time of King Louis XIV, asparagus was dubbed 'King of Vegetables'. Common asparagus varieties include green asparagus, violet or purple asparagus, and wild asparagus. Fresh asparagus has crisp, plump stems with their slightly purple tips still intact. Asparagus is available fresh, frozen and canned. Fresh asparagus is available all year round in most markets.

Avocado

Avocado symbolises richness, abundance and continuity of life. It is also known as alligator pear due to the pebbly, rough exterior of the common variety of this fruit. The pear shape and its rich sensuous flavour and texture assure the avocado its pride of place amongsts aphrodisiacs. The pale yellow-green flesh of the avocado has a smooth and buttery texture and faintly nutty flavour. It is commonly used in salads and the highly popular guacamole dip, as well as in breads, desserts and main dishes. When exposed to air, the fruit of the avocado darkens. Therefore, it is necessary to work quickly once it has been cut. One way to avoid this discolouration is to add lemon juice to a cut avocado.

Beetroot

Aphrodite, the Goddess of Love, believed in the power of the heart-shaped beetroot to enhance beauty and love. Beetroots must be the inspiration for Tom Robbins' *Jitterbug Perfume* which is a journey in search of immortality, love and self-reliance. Native to the Mediterranean, this vegetable's juice was considered an aphrodisiac by the Romans. It caught the attention of the French only in the 1800s, even though the leaves were being eaten for centuries earlier. Beetroot is generally deep ruby-red in colour, though its other colours range from yellow to white, and even candy-striped (with red and white concentric circles) called Chioggia, available in specialty markets. The rich maroon flesh of this root vegetable is naturally sweet tasting, nutritious and has an earthy flavour. Beetroot powder is used as a colouring agent for many foods. Beetroots are available all year round and the best ones have firm and smooth skin. Small or medium-sized beetroots are generally more tender than the large ones.

Cardamom

Cardamom is an expensive spice, third only to saffron and is also known as the festive spice. It is mentioned in Greek literature of 4th century BC. In *The Indian Spice Kitchen*, Monisha Bharadwaj writes that Mughal emperors carried cardamom pods in silver boxes as mouth fresheners. Cardamom was also used in perfumes by ancient Greeks and Romans. It has been mentioned as an aphrodisiac in *The Arabian Nights* as well as the *Kama Sutra*. It is said that Cleopatra used a blend of cardamom, rose, and cinnamon to entice Mark Antony. In Deepa Mehta's film, *Fire*, Sita asks Radha, 'What do brides eat on their wedding night?' Radha replies, 'They eat green cardamom for fragrance.' There are three types of cardamom: green, black and white, the green cardamom being the most popular. The green cardamom has a rich, lemony flavour with an intense aroma. The pod itself is neutral in flavour and generally not used. It adds bitterness to the dishes when left in. Cardamoms can be used whole or split in Indian cooking, or the seeds can be bruised and fried before adding the main ingredients to the pan. It can also be pounded with other spices as required. In India, cardamom is the main ingredient in many recipes of the spice mixture *garam masala*. It is especially prized for curries and pilafs in northern India and Pakistan. Cardamom is best stored in pod form, because when the seeds are exposed or ground, they lose their flavour soon after.

Celery

Celery originates from the Mediterranean and the Middle East. It was considered a holy plant in ancient Greece. It was worn by the winners of the Nemean Games – one of the four games of ancient Greece – like bay leaves worn at the Olympic Games. There are two types of celery – the yellow or the self-blanching variety and the green variety. Green celery is the preferred choice in North America while in Europe and the rest of the world, the self-blanching variety is more commonly eaten. Celery has a mild acid content that gives it a tangy flavour. It is sharper than a sweet pepper.

Chilli Peppers

Chilli peppers are native to South and Central America and were named 'peppers' by the European explorer Christopher Columbus because they are similar to black peppers. Chilli peppers are considered aphrodisiacs because of the presence of 'capsaicin', responsible for the heat in the chillies, stimulating our nerve ends and producing a natural high. Chilli peppers come in different sizes, colours and heat/flavour, ranging from mild to moderately hot and extremely hot. They also come in a several forms – fresh, pickled, smoked, dried, roasted, and ground. The best ones are smooth, shiny and firm skinned. Usually the smaller-sized chillies are the hotter ones. Since the heat of the chilli pepper is mostly contained in the seeds, wearing gloves while handling chilli peppers is recommended. Some of the heat of the chilli pepper can be reduced by removing the ribs or veins and soaking it in cold, salty water or vinegar for half a minute.

Chocolate

Chocolate is the undisputed king of aphrodisiacs. The literal meaning of its name chocolate translates to 'Food of the Gods'. It is believed that Casanova was a great chocolate fanatic. The first people said to have made chocolate were from ancient Mexico and central America. The Mayans and the Aztecs – mixed ground seeds from the cacao tree with seasoning to make a tasty and frothy drink. Pure chocolate is unsweetened, consisting of cocoa solids and cocoa butter. Most of the chocolate consumed is sweet chocolate – chocolate combined with sugar. Milk, white and dark are the popular varieties of chocolate. Milk chocolate is sweet chocolate, which in addition to sugar, contains milk powder or condensed milk. Good chocolate should be smooth and not grainy when eaten, literally melting in your mouth. Chocolate from different manufacturers tastes different, its taste finally depending on where the cacao beans originated from, how they were roasted and the proportions in which cocoa butter, sugar and pure chocolate were mixed.

Cilantro/Coriander

Cilantro is mentioned in the Bible as one of the plants that grew in the Hanging Gardens of Babylon. The ancient Hebrews added it to a herb mixture used in the Passover

rituals. The Chinese used this herb in love potions believing that it made one immortal. Derived from the leaves (and stems) of the coriander plant, cilantro has a very fresh, pungent aroma and a tangy parsley and lemony citrus taste. It is very popular in Chinese, Indian, Arab, and Latin American cooking. In Indian cooking, cilantro is used in a lot of dishes as an ingredient as well as a garnish, sprinkled whole or as chopped leaves, just before serving as heating reduces its flavour. Cilantro can be usually found fresh in the local grocery store and is available all year round. The best cilantro has bright green leaves with an even colour.

Cinnamon

The poem, *Cinnamon Peeler,* by the Booker Prize winning novelist Michael Ondaatje, is an exploration of friendship, love and passion using the exotic qualities of cinnamon. Native to Ceylon or Sri Lanka, cinnamon in red wine was part of Roman traditions, and considered favourable for women as well as men. Cinnamon bark is widely used as a spice. The two varieties of cinnamon are – Chinese and Sri Lankan. Cinnamon from Sri Lanka is slightly more sweet and refined while the cassia or the Chinese variety is less expensive. Cinnamon is grown in various parts of southern India, especially in Kerala. True cinnamon sticks or quills will be curled in a tubular form, while cassia quills curl inwards from both sides, like a scroll. True cinnamon is tan in colour while ground cassia is reddish brown and usually coarser in texture. The bold and spicy, sweet-warm taste of cinnamon is used extensively in baked goods, cakes, desserts as well as in marinades, and for cooking meats and stews. It is added to chocolate as a flavouring as well as in liquors and bitters.

Cucumber

Cucumber originated in India and from there, spread to Greece, Italy and China. These cool, crisp and juicy vegetables are a popular aphrodisiac. Table cucumber is usually served raw in salads, sandwiches and drinks. Pickling cucumbers are usually smaller than table cucumbers, and often have a thick warty peel. Smaller, firm, unblemished cucumbers have a better flavour. Firm, unblemished cucumbers that are rounded at the tips and heavy for their size are the best, unlike those with soft spots or withered ends. Small and slender cucumbers usually have a better flavour and fewer seeds. The tips, peels and seeds should be removed as they may be bitter. Cucumber can be seeded by cutting it lengthwise and scraping the seeds out with a knife or a spoon.

Dates

The fruit of the date palm is known as a date. It is considered the 'Sacred Fruit of the Arabs'. Dates, a symbol of grace and elegance, are mixed with milk and cinnamon to make a popular aphrodisiac. Dates, the world's oldest cultivated fruits, are highly nutritious and can be eaten whole or pitted and stuffed with other nuts. They are also added to salads and roast chicken. Ripe dates are brown in colour and like prunes, have a shrivelled skin. Fresh and plump, dates with an even colour taste the best. During the month of Ramadan, Muslims all around the world break their fast each evening with dates.

Eggs

Eggs are a symbol of fertility and creation of new life since the times of ancient Greece and the *Kama Sutra*. The custom of hanging red eggs in evergreen trees, originating in Germany, is another powerful ancient symbol of rebirth and renewal. At the end of Lent, all the eggs saved up during the 40 days were used in the Easter omelette. Hand-decorated eggs are also exchanged at springtime and on Easter. The most commonly used eggs are those from the chicken. Duck and goose eggs, and smaller ones such as quail eggs are also used as a gourmet ingredient, as are the largest bird eggs, of ostriches. Chicken eggs are used in many types of dishes, both sweet and savoury. Eggs can be prepared in a variety of ways – pickled, hard-boiled, soft-boiled, scrambled, fried and refrigerated. Quail eggs are considered a delicacy in many countries.

Fennel

Fennel is one of the oldest cultivated plants valued by the Romans, taken by warriors for good health. Fennel was considered an aphrodisiac even in ancient Egyptian times. Greeks and Hindus believed in its power too. A Hindu aphrodisiac recipe includes fennel juice, honey, ghee (clarified butter), sugar and liquorice. The leaves and seeds of fennel are used to impart a nutty liquorice-like flavour and aroma to recipes, while the crispy, sweet stalk is eaten like a vegetable, in salads. Since heat dilutes the flavour very quickly, fennel is added late in the cooking process. It is one of Italy's most popular vegetables. Chopped fennel is very popular in tomato-based sauces.

Fenugreek

Fenugreek was a favourite of the Greek physician, Hippocrates, who valued it for its soothing properties. It is native to North Africa and the eastern Mediterranean. Fenugreek has had the reputation for enhancing libido and is included in the list of aphrodisiacs. Fenugreek is available in the form of seeds, and the leaves too are used. The seeds are hard and have a bitter taste and a spicy aroma. Roasting and grinding helps reduce the bitterness. The crushed seeds are added to make curry powder. They are commonly used in marinades, pickles, and condiments and on breads in countries like India, Egypt and Ethiopia. Dried leaves of the fenugreek plant add a wonderful aroma and flavour to breads and curries.

Garlic

According to *Symbolism of Herbs* by Richters, garlic stands for protection, strength and healing. In ancient times, it was highly prized. Egyptians worshipped it and placed clay models of garlic bulbs in the tomb of Tutankhamen. Along with the Greeks they embraced garlic's aphrodisiac properties. It is available fresh, as peeled cloves, powdered or as dehydrated flakes. Of all varieties, the white-skinned garlic is the most popular. The other varieties are the Mexican and the Italian garlic which have a milder flavour and mauve-coloured skin. Garlic is one of the most popular herbs used in cooking today and adds a pungent flavour to sauces, meats and soups. It can be used in various ways to control the amount released during the cooking process – by pressing, crushing, mincing, chopping, slicing or browning. Pressing releases the maximum flavour and slicing the least. Firm, plump bulbs with a dry, papery covering are the freshest.

Goji Berries

Wolfberries or goji berries originate from the Himalayan region; the Chinese believed that goji berries were the fruit of immortality. Even in present times, this fruit is highly valued for its health benefits thanks to its high levels of antioxidants. In parts of Tibet, goji berry is referred to as the 'laughing berry'. Goji berries look similar to raisins though they are red in colour and slightly more pointed and have a salty/sour taste. They are used in cooking savoury stews of chicken, pork, and wine is made from the juice of these berries. Dried goji berries are used in trail mixes and salads, and are readily available in health food stores.

Honey

The word 'aphrodisiac' comes from the name of the Greek Goddess of Love, Aphrodite. Honey is also known as the 'Nectar of Aphrodite'. Lovers on their honeymoon drank mead to sweeten their marriage. Mead is honey wine; it was the first alcoholic drink ever brewed (even before wine or beer) and it was thought to sweeten a marriage. Both the *Kama Sutra* and *The Perfumed Garden* mention a recipe of honey and nutmeg. The flavour of honey can range from mild to spicy or fragrant, and can often be a combination of one or more flavours. The colours can vary from white to yellow, to gold, dark brown, red and even black. The lighter the colour of the honey, the milder the flavour; the darker-hued ones have a deeper, more robust flavour. Honey is a natural organic substitute for sugar and can be stored indefinitely. When added to baked goods, it remain fresh longer because of its moisture content. As honey is twice as sweet as sugar and contains water, adjustments have to be made to the quantity and amount of water that needs to be added to recipes. Honey is available in various forms – liquid, solid or comb. If honey crystallises and becomes cloudy, reheating it can help make it clear again.

Mangoes

This 'King of Fruits' originated in northeast India and its surrounding regions and is mentioned in the Vedas. Mango leaves are used for decoration in auspicious ceremonies and its blossoms signify abundance and divinity. The mango tree is a symbol of love and believed to grant wishes. It is the national fruit of India, Bangladesh and the Philippines. This tropical fruit has a moist flesh which surrounds a large inedible seed. It is the preferred choice in fruits because of its distinct aroma and sweet-and sour-flavour. Mangoes are available fresh or dried, as well as canned, and come in a variety of colours – yellowish, reddish, greenish. The best way to select a ripe mango is by its smell, which should be full and fruity at the stem end. If the mango is soft to touch when lightly squeezed, then it is good to eat. Though the colour of mangoes can vary, the yellow-coloured ones are the best-tasting. The larger the fruit, the greater the flesh to seed ratio. Dried mangoes must be rehydrated in warm water for about four hours before use.

Mint

'Mint' comes from the Latin word, 'mentha', which in turn comes from the Greek word 'minthe'. Minthe was a Greek mythological nymph who was transformed into the mint plant by Pluto's wife. Since Pluto could not undo the spell, he softened it by giving the plant a sweet aromatic fragrance which would perfume the air. It was regarded as a symbol of hospitality, and strewn around by the Romans while welcoming their guests. The great thinker Aristotle advised Alexander the Great against allowing mint tea during campaigns because he believed it to be an aphrodisiac. Mint is a very popular herb; the leaves give dishes a fresh aromatic sweet, tangy flavour with a cool aftertaste. It is used in teas, jellies, salads, syrups, candies, and also to flavour or garnish alcoholic drinks. Mint is one of the staple herbs used in cooking; its strong flavour adds freshness to recipes. Different varieties of mint – spearmint, applemint, peppermint, and many more, add varying flavours depending on how strong the desired result is. Spearmint imparts the strongest mint flavour while the flavour of chopped applemint is not as overpowering.

Mushroom

Ancient Egyptian scriptures show that mushrooms were reserved only for the Pharaohs as they were believed to impart immortality. Thus only kings could partake of the munificence of mushrooms. They are considered a powerful aphrodisiac by many cultures because of their taste and earthy aroma. In the 11th century, the Normans fed them to the groom on the day of the wedding. Some of the exotic varieties include shiitake, enoki, oyster, morels, cèpes, and chanterelles. Each mushroom variety has its own flavour, but the varieties can be substituted for one another in most recipes. Care should be taken to ensure that the toxic, inedible ones are not used in cooking. Fresh mushrooms have a porous texture and are never soaked; soft brushing is usually the best way to clean mushrooms. Dried mushrooms are available and are ready to be used in recipes after they are soaked in hot water for 10-20 minutes. Mushrooms are a versatile ingredient and can be sautéed, stir-fried, roasted or even grilled. They can be eaten raw, or cooked – whole or sliced. Using a variety of mushrooms in the recipe rather than just one kind enhances the taste of mushrooms in the dish. The best mushrooms are firm and evenly coloured with clear, blemish-free caps.

Nutmeg

The history of nutmeg goes back to the 1st century as evidenced by writings of Roman philosophers, and was extremely expensive till a few hundred years ago. This spice has been prized by Arabs, Greeks, Indians and Romans as an aphrodisiac. In India, a combination of nutmeg, honey and a half-boiled egg is eaten. Chinese women believed that nutmeg contributed to fertility. In Ayurveda, nutmeg is considered a stronger aphrodisiac than spices like cinnamon. Nutmeg is actually the seed of an evergreen tree which produces both nutmeg and mace. The sweet, nutty flavours of nutmeg are added to sauces, drinks, eggnogs. It adds a warm aroma to Indian savoury dishes, especially Mughlai cuisine. Nutmeg is available whole or ground. Whole is preferable as the flavour of ground nutmeg deteriorates fast. A pinch or two of nutmeg is enough to add flavour to a recipe.

Oysters

Oysters, the world's classic love food, were first recognised for their aphrodisiac properties by the Romans. It is said that Casanova ate 50 raw oysters every morning. Combined with wine, the flavour of oysters enhances the senses and is an important part of a great romantic evening. The most effective way to open oysters is with an oyster knife. The pointed end of a knife can be used to pry open the shells that are joined together, and also to remove the oyster from its shell. The liquid inside the oysters needs to be preserved. The flavour of oysters can vary from salty with hints of cucumber, to melon or herbs depending upon the water in which they grow. Oysters are one of the most nutritionally well-balanced foods. They are best served raw with crushed ice and seaweed so as to retain their delicate flavour. Common accompaniments are lemon juice and/ or Worchestershire sauce. Since oysters are naturally salty, the amount of salt needs to be adjusted when using them in a recipe. The meat of younger and smaller oysters is more tender; they should be cooked gently to avoid the meat becoming tough.

Peaches

Peaches originated in China and were a favourite fruit of emperors. The old name for peach is 'Persian Apple'. During the reign of Queen Victoria, no meal was complete without peaches served in handkerchiefs. In Japan, brides hold peach blossoms in celebration of fertility. Chinese folklore speaks of the 'Peach Tree of the Gods', which blossomed once every 3000 years. The fruit it bore was said to grant health and virility to those who consumed it. Peaches can be of two varieties: the clingstone, used in canned peaches, where the flesh of the fruit clings to the stone; freestone, which is available in grocery stores, where the stone easily separates from the fruit. Both kinds are available in white and yellow varieties – the white variety is sweeter and less acidic than the yellow variety. The skin around the fruit is fuzzy, yet edible. To remove the skin, the fruit should be blanched in boiling water for a minute and then dipped into cold water, which will make the skin slip off easily. Fragrant peaches with firm, unblemished skin are best for making popular recipes like cobblers, pies and melbas.

Black Peppercorns

Black peppercorn, a widely acknowledged aphrodisiac was an extremely valuable and a rare spice, and was even used as currency in ancient times. This spice inspired numerous sailing expeditions which were undertaken to find a route to the Far East where this spice was available. Black pepper in one form or other is used around the world to flavour both savoury and sweet dishes. There are three types of peppercorns – black, white and green, the most common being the black peppercorn. Having the strongest flavour of the three, it is slightly hot with a hint of sweetness. Black and white peppercorns are available whole, cracked and coarsely or finely ground. Tellicherry and Lampong are the best varieties of black peppercorns.

Passion Fruit

First grown by the Aztecs, this aromatic fruit tantalises the senses and has an overall calming effect on its consumer. There are two main varieties of passion fruit: the golden-yellow passion fruit which is similar to a large orange, and the more commonly known variety, the purple passion fruit, with a small wrinkled skin – an indication that the fruit is ripe and ready to eat. On the inside, the fragrant flesh is golden with blackish, pinkish seeds which are edible. The taste of the fruit is a combination of orange, pineapple and guava. The best passion fruits are the fresh ones with a perfume-like aroma. The fruit can be eaten by splitting it and scooping out the flesh. The juice mixed with a little sugar makes a wonderful dressing for salads and as an ingredient in cocktails.

Pine Nuts

Pine nuts have been a staple in Italian cuisine since the days of ancient Rome. These nuts have been used as an aphrodisiac throughout the Mediterranean and the East. *The Perfumed Garden,* an ancient Arabic love manual, contains many references to pine nuts. A popular recipe in this book is a glass of honey with 20 almonds and 100 pine nuts to be consumed for three consecutive nights. Sweet buttery flavoured pine nuts are the edible seeds of pine trees. They must be lightly toasted to enhance their flavour and make them a little crunchy. They are used extensively in cooking, as salad toppings and in pestoes and meat, fish and vegetable recipes. Pine nuts are mostly sold pre-shelled. Seeds in the shell are more likely to last longer.

Pomegranate

Indian royalty began their banquets with pomegranates, grapes, and jujubes. Traditionally, they represent fertility and prosperity. The beauty of the pomegranate has inspired design since time immemorial and led to the belief that this is the 'Fruit of Paradise'. The pomegranate has appeared innumerable times in the works of great writers such as Homer and Shakespeare. In *Mughal-e-Azam*, one of the greatest love stories in Indian cinema, the heroine in the saga, was named Anarkali – 'Blossoming Pomegranate', as a tribute to her exceptional beauty. The flavour of the pomegranate is sweet, yet tarty. The skin is tough and wrinkled, but inside are bright red ruby-like seeds. The seeds are the only edible part of the fruit. The sweet, tangy flavourful juice is used as a base for sauces, drinks, desserts, as well as savoury dishes. The seeds can be eaten alone or used as a colourful garnish. Grenadine syrup made from pomegranate juice is a great addition to alcoholic drinks or cocktails.

Rose

Named the 'Queen of Love' by Aphrodite, it was created by the Goddess of Flowers – Chloris. The colour red has always been associated with life and deep emotions, making the red rose a universal symbol of love and fidelity. Even today, red roses are an integral part of the celebration of love, especially on Valentine's Day. The scent of the rose is considered a classic aphrodisiac for women. Cleopatra was known to have used a special blend of rose, cardamom, and cinnamon to seduce Mark Antony. Roses have been used in cooking as well as in decoration. The flavour of roses is subtle and sweet, with spicy undertones. The deeper the colour of the rose, the deeper the flavour it will impart to the food. The edible parts of the rose – hips, petals and shoots – are used for making marmalades, jams and syrups. Small amounts of rosewater are used to add a warm and sweet rose scent to food. Crushed, dried rose petals are used in spice blends for flavouring recipes. Rose syrup is diluted to make a cool, refreshing drink in the Middle East and the Indian subcontinent.

Rosemary

The Latin meaning of rosemary is 'Dew of the Sea' or 'Sea Foam'. Aphrodite was born from sea foam. Rosemary is a symbol of remembrance and faithfulness, and is added to a wedding bouquet. In early times, rosemary represented the dominance of the woman in the house where it was grown. A necklace made from rosemary is believed to preserve youth. Rosemary was one of the cordial herbs used to flavour ale and wine. Because of its captivating aroma, it is considered a powerful aphrodisiac. It has a pine-like fragrance and its pungent flavour is used in chicken, lamb, pork, salmon and tuna dishes. It is an indispensable herb in cooking. Usually rosemary leaves are used in cooking, traditionally more so in Mediterranean cooking, but at times the entire rosemary sprig can be used as a seasoning. The smell and flavour of burnt rosemary is similar to that of the flavour and smell of barbecuing.

Saffron

Saffron finds its root in the Arabic word 'Zà faran', meaning yellow. The foundation of eternal love is always selflessness. The deep yellow/orange colour of the robes of sages and saints, also the colour of saffron represents sacrifice and divine love. Saffron is obtained from the deep yellow stamens of the purple flower, Crocus sativus. It is the most expensive spice in the world as it takes 75,000 blossoms to make one pound of spice. Its unique bitter-honey taste is used in cuisines across the world, especially those of the Middle East. Saffron should be steeped in water before cooking, to release more flavour and colour. Saffron preparations are considered an elixir which creates a state of wellness and good mood. Saffron grows all over the world; the quality and flavour depends upon the region it is grown in. The best saffron comes from Spain and Kashmir.

Tomatoes

Tomatoes originated in Southern and Central America, and date back to the times of the early Aztecs. The Italians were the first to adopt and cultivate the tomato outside this region. They came to be known by the French as *pommes d'amour*, or love apples, as they are said to have aphrodisiac properties. Fresh, ripe tomatoes are very popular even today. They add a deep colour and large amounts of vitamin C to food. Tomatoes have a high acidic content which makes them ideal for canning. Sun-dried tomatoes – plum tomatoes in olive oil – are an important ingredient in many modern recipes. Among the many varieties of tomatoes available in different sizes and colours, the best known are beefsteak, plum, grape, baby romas, and the small red or yellow cherry tomatoes. As they tend to become soft and mushy fast and loose their flavour, tomatoes should be purchased fresh in small quantities.

Vanilla

Originally from Mexico, vanilla is used predominately in sweet dishes. The Aztecs revered this spice and gifted vanilla beans to their emperor who was worshipped as a god, as a tribute. They valued this spice in the same way that they valued cocoa. They used vanilla mixed with chocolate as an aphrodisiac. Vanilla is an orchid. Most of the 60 species available around the world are not suited for producing vanilla beans. Hence, vanilla is a very expensive spice, second only to saffron. The aphrodisiac qualities of vanilla come from its black beans, not just from the taste but also from the scent, which is sweet and enticing. It is used extensively in perfumes, floral bouquets, and in calming scents. Vanilla is available in liquid form or as long thin pods. It is used for flavouring milk, puddings, baked goods, and drinks too.

Yams

Cultivated for centuries in Africa and Asia, certain yams like the Brazilian wild yam have traditionally been considered an aphrodisiac. They are often mistaken for sweet potatoes, but are a completely different vegetable. Generally, yams can be used in place of sweet potatoes in any recipe. Yams with tight, unblemished skin, taste the best – earthy, with a minimal amount of sweetness. There are many kinds of yams, and their colours vary from white, ivory, yellow, purple to brownish-black. With a starchy texture and an earthy, deep taste, yams complement darker meats such as venison.

Soups

Broccoli Romanesco and Mushroom–Black Pepper Soup

Serves 4

Ingredients

4 small broccoli Romanesco
4 tablespoons unsalted butter
2 cloves garlic, coarsely chopped
1½ pounds oyster mushrooms or any other variety, thinly sliced
4 cups vegetable stock
½ cup heavy cream
Freshly ground black pepper
Salt to taste

Directions

In a medium-sized pan, bring 2 cups salted water to a boil and cook the broccoli Romanesco for about 2 to 3 minutes until tender. Drain the water and keep warm.

In a heavy-bottomed saucepan, heat the butter over medium to high heat until the foam subsides. Add the garlic and stir continuously until golden brown.

Add the mushrooms and sauté for 4 to 5 minutes or until the liquid in the pan evaporates and the mushrooms begin to brown.

Add 4 cups of stock and salt to taste. Simmer for 2 minutes. Purée the soup in batches in a blender and pour back into the pot. Add ½ cup of cream and simmer for another 2 to 3 minutes.

Place the broccoli Romanesco in the centre of the soup bowl and pour the soup around it. Serve hot, sprinkled with freshly ground black pepper.

Beetroot-Citron Soup with Nutmeg

Serves 4

Ingredients

2 tablespoons canola oil

3 medium beetroots, peeled and cut into ½-inch cubes

2 cloves garlic, finely chopped

1 tablespoon flour

½ cup unsweetened coconut milk

1 teaspoon grated rind of Buddha's fingers citron
  or any variety of lemon

½ teaspoon ground nutmeg

1½ cup vegetable stock

4 small slices of spice-crusted bread such as a crispy baguette

4 sprigs of thyme

Salt to taste

Directions

Heat the oil in a large saucepan over medium to high heat and add the beetroot, garlic and flour, and sauté. Stir continuously for about 5 minutes until the garlic is golden brown.

Add the coconut milk, grated rind, nutmeg, salt, and stock, and bring to a boil. Lower the heat and simmer for 15 to 20 minutes until the beetroots are cooked.

Remove 8 cubes of beetroot and cut them into small dices, and reserve for garnish.

Serve the soup hot, topped with bread slices, beetroot dices and thyme.

Avocado Soup
with Spicy Salsa

Serves 4

Ingredients

1 vine-ripened red tomato
1 large red onion, finely chopped
2 tablespoons coarsely chopped fresh cilantro
1 fresh Serrano or jalapeño chilli, seeded and chopped
Juice of 2 limes
4 ripe Haas avocados, peeled, pitted and cut into chunks
2 tablespoons vegetable oil
3 cloves garlic, chopped
1 quart vegetable stock; more, if required
Salt to taste

Directions

Quarter and seed the tomato. Dice and transfer it to a bowl. Stir in half of the chopped onions, cilantro, Serrano chilli, salt, and half the lime juice. Cover the bowl and put it into the refrigerator.

In a large non-reactive mixing bowl, toss the avocados with the remaining lime juice until
evenly coated.

Heat the oil in a large saucepan over medium to high heat and add the remaining onions and garlic, and sauté. Stir continuously for about 5 minutes until the onions are translucent.

Add salt, avocados and stock. Bring to a boil, then reduce heat and simmer for 8 to 10 minutes.

Remove from heat and purée in a blender, adding more stock if the mixture is too thick.

Refrigerate and serve chilled, topped with tomato salsa.

Ginger, Spinach and Yogurt Soup

Serves 4

Ingredients

2 tablespoons olive oil
1 large onion, finely chopped
1 (2-inch) piece fresh ginger, peeled and finely chopped
2 cloves garlic, finely chopped
1 chilli, such as Serrano, seeded and finely chopped
2 (28-ounce) cans coconut milk
2 cups vegetable stock
½ cup heavy cream
1 cup low fat unsweetened yogurt, whisked until smooth
1½ cups coarsely chopped baby spinach (about 1 ounce)
1 bunch chives
Salt to taste

Directions

Heat the oil in a large saucepan over medium to high heat and add onions, ginger, garlic and chilli.

Sauté for 5 minutes, stirring continuously until the onions are translucent.

Add the coconut milk, vegetable stock, heavy cream, and bring to a boil.

Gently add the yogurt, little at a time, and cook for another 3 minutes.

Stir in the spinach and season with salt, and simmer for another 2 to 3 minutes.

Divide and tie the chives into bunches, and serve it with the soup.

Butternut Squash with Cinnamon and Oregano

Serves 4

Ingredients

1 medium (about 2 pounds) butternut squash
3 tablespoons unsalted butter
2 medium shallots, coarsely chopped
1 (2-inch) cinnamon stick
1 tablespoon freshly grated ginger
6 cups chicken broth
1 cup water, or as needed
4 sprigs of oregano
Salt and pepper to taste

Directions

Peel the butternut squash and cut into half. Scoop out the seeds and cut into 1-inch chunks.

In a large heavy-bottomed saucepan, heat the butter over medium to high heat and add the shallots, cinnamon, and ginger, and sauté, stirring continuously until the shallots begin to turn golden brown.

Add the chopped squash and stock and bring to a boil. Cover and simmer for 15 to 20 minutes until the squash is tender.

Transfer the mixture to a blender or food processor, and purée the mixture in batches until smooth. Add enough water to achieve the desired consistency, and salt and pepper to taste. Return the soup to the saucepan and cook over moderate heat until it is hot.

Garnish each portion with a sprig of oregano.

Saffron, Radish and Tomato Soup

Serves 4

Ingredients

1 bunch fresh radishes (about 1 pound)
1 tablespoon vegetable oil
½ cup chopped carrot
2 cloves garlic, minced
2 (28 ounce) cans crushed tomatoes
2 tablespoons all-purpose flour
4 cups low-sodium vegetable broth
½ teaspoon dried thyme
1 teaspoon saffron strands, plus a pinch for garnish
1 cup water, or as needed
¼ cup heavy cream
Salt to taste

Directions

Clean and trim the radishes, discarding the greens. Cut them into half, reserving one for the garnish.

In a Dutch oven, heat the oil over medium heat. Add the radishes, carrots, garlic, and season with salt. Cook, stirring continuously, for about 3 minutes until the radishes are tender. Stir in the tomatoes and flour, and cook for another 2 minutes.

Add the broth, thyme and 1 teaspoon saffron and bring to a boil. Cover and simmer for about 10 minutes until the mixture is well combined.

Transfer the mixture to a blender or food processor, and purée the mixture in batches until smooth. Add enough water to achieve the desired consistency. Return the soup to the saucepan and stir in the heavy cream and cook over moderate heat until it is hot.

Thinly slice the reserved radish and garnish the soup, topped with a slice of radish and a pinch of saffron.

Wild Rice and Celery Soup

Serves 4

Ingredients

8 ribs celery
2 medium carrots
2 tablespoons vegetable oil
1 small onion, finely chopped
1 tablespoon flour
4 cups chicken stock, heated
1 cup wild rice, cooked
3 tablespoons grated cheddar cheese
Salt to taste

Directions

Trim the celery and cut into ½- to 1-inch pieces.

Peel the carrots and cut them into ¼- to ½-inch dices.

Heat the oil in a Dutch oven over medium heat and add the onion
and sauté, stirring continuously for about 5 minutes until the onions
are translucent.

Add the celery, carrots, and salt, stirring continuously for about 5
minutes until the carrots are tender.

Stir in the flour, and continue cooking, stirring for 1 minute.
Whisk in the hot stock and bring to a boil. Reduce heat and simmer for
about 10 minutes. Stir in the wild rice and bring the soup to a boil.

Serve with grated cheese.

Salads

Apricots, Almonds and Mesclun Salad

Serves 4 to 6

Ingredients

¼ cup extra virgin olive oil
1½ tablespoons rice vinegar
1 teaspoon Dijon mustard
1 (2-inch) piece fresh ginger, peeled and finely chopped
2 garlic cloves, minced
2 tablespoons coarsely chopped fresh cilantro
4 cups (about ¼ pound) mesclun, rinsed and spun dry
2 ripe apricots, pitted and quartered
16 almonds
Freshly ground black pepper
Salt to taste

Directions

Combine oil, vinegar, salt, and mustard in a mixer and blend for about 30 seconds until a creamy emulsion forms.

In a small mixing bowl, add ginger, garlic and cilantro to the emulsion and mix well. Cover and refrigerate.

Combine the mesclun, apricots, and almonds in a large non-reactive mixing bowl. Gently drizzle the vinaigrette and toss the salad until evenly coated. Serve with freshly ground black pepper.

Goji Berries and Spicy Indian Cheese Salad

Serves 4

Ingredients

1 litre whole milk
2 to 3 tablespoons lemon juice
Vegetable oil for frying
¼ cup goji berries, or any dried berries
1 medium red onion, finely chopped
1 jalapeño cut into ⅛-inch rings
Juice of 1 lemon
1 tablespoon coarsely chopped flat-leaf parsley
Salt to taste

Directions

Bring the milk to a temperature just below boiling point, then turn the heat off. Add lemon juice, 1 tablespoon at a time and keep stirring the milk after each addition until the milk curdles. Remove from heat when the solid curd separate from the whey.

Line a strainer with a cheese-cloth and strain the mixture. Rinse the curd with fresh water. Squeeze out the moisture from the curd by pressing it, and reserve.

Wrapping it tightly with the cloth, form the shape of a block. Tie a knot and place the cheese-cloth under some heavy weight like a pile of books or a brick for at least 15 minutes until the cheese (Indian *paneer*) is set. Remove from the cheese-cloth and cut the cheese into 1-inch cubes.

Heat the oil to 350° F and gently fry the paneer in batches until lightly browned at the edges. Remove and drain on a kitchen towel.

In a large mixing bowl, combine the *paneer,* goji berries, onions, jalapeño, lemon juice, parsley, and salt.

Serve at room temperature.

Crispy Okra Salad with Dried Mango Strips

Serves 4

Ingredients

1 pound fresh okra
Vegetable oil, enough for deep frying
1 teaspoon dried mango powder
1 teaspoon red chilli flakes
½ small red onion, very thinly sliced
3 tablespoons coarsely chopped cilantro
Juice of 1 lemon
1 sheet (about 2 ounces) of dried mango slice, cut into thin strips
Salt to taste

Directions

Rinse the okra and pat dry thoroughly with a kitchen towel. Trim the tops and cut lengthwise into thin strips

In a large, deep skillet, heat the vegetable oil to 350° F. Working in batches, fry the okra strips for about 4 minutes, stirring a few times until golden and crisp. Using a slotted spoon, transfer the fried okra to a large paper-towel-lined plate to drain excess oil. Sprinkle with some of the salt, dried mango powder and red chilli flakes.

In a large bowl, gently toss the fried okra with the red onion, cilantro and lemon juice. Season the salad with more of the spice mixture and salt, and serve immediately, garnished with dried mango strips.

Dried Lily Buds-Brussel Sprouts in Pepper-Lemon Dressing

Serves 4

Ingredients

¼ teaspoon finely grated fresh lemon zest
Juice of 1 lemon
Freshly ground black pepper
1 teaspoon sugar
1 tablespoon olive oil
½ cup dried lily buds
1 pound Brussels sprouts
1 medium red onion, cut into ½-inch dices
1 medium-ripe tomato, seeded and coarsely chopped
Salt to taste

Directions

Whisk together the zest, lemon juice, pepper, sugar and salt until the sugar and salt dissolve. Add the oil in a slow stream, whisking until emulsified. Cover and refrigerate.

Soak the dried lily buds in warm water for 15 minutes. Rinse, dry and cut off and discard any hard ends of the buds.

Trim the base of the Brussels sprouts, then slice them in half or, if large, into quarters.

Bring a large pot of water to a boil, and add 1 tablespoon salt. Add the Brussels sprouts and cook for about 5 minutes until tender. Drain and pat dry with a kitchen towel to remove any excess water.

In a large mixing bowl, combine the dried lily buds, sprouts, onion, and tomato and gently drizzle the dressing to evenly coat the ingredients.

Serve fresh.

Mixed Sprouts with Pomegranate Vinaigrette

Serves 4

Ingredients

3 tablespoons pomegranate juice
2 tablespoons red wine vinegar
1 tablespoon honey
1 teaspoon Dijon mustard
Freshly ground black pepper
¼ cup olive oil
2 cups fresh mixed sprouts
Salt to taste

Directions

Whisk together pomegranate juice, vinegar, honey, mustard, salt and pepper until all the ingredients are well combined. Add oil in a slow stream, whisking until emulsified. Cover and refrigerate.

Toss the sprouts with the vinaigrette until well coated. Serve fresh.

Mustard Seeds-Infused Warm Yams with Upland Cress

Serves 4

Ingredients
3 medium yams, peeled and cubed
2 tablespoons vegetable or canola oil
1 tablespoon mustard seeds
3 cloves garlic, finely chopped
Juice of 1 lemon
1 bunch fresh upland cress
Salt to taste

Directions
In a large saucepan, cook the yams for 8 to 10 minutes in salted boiling water until tender. Drain and keep warm.

In the saucepan heat the oil on medium heat and fry the mustard seeds and garlic, stirring continuously for about 2 minutes until very fragrant.

Add the yams, lemon juice and, season with salt. Stir until well combined.

Serve warm on a bed of upland cress.

Asafoetida-Crusted Scallops with Arugula and Star Anise

Serves 4 to 6

Ingredients

10 to 12 large sea scallops (about 1 pound) tough muscles removed
1 teaspoon asafoetida
3 tablespoons olive oil
3 star anise
Juice of 1 lemon
4 cups young arugula leaves, rinsed and dried
2 tablespoons pumpkin seeds, lightly toasted
Salt to taste

Directions

Gently pat the scallops dry with paper towels. In a food storage bag, toss the scallops gently with asafoetida, 1 tablespoon olive oil, and salt. Refrigerate for about 1 hour.

Heat the remaining 2 tablespoons olive oil in a large skillet over high heat. Add the star anise and fry for about 1 minute until very fragrant.

With tongs, arrange the scallops in the hot oil and cook for about 2 to 3 minutes on each side, or until golden brown.

Remove and drain excess oil on a kitchen towel.

Remove the oil from heat and stir in the lemon juice and cool.

Toss the arugula in the reserved oil and divide the salad onto plates topped with the scallops and pumpkin seeds.

Fish & Shellfish

Mussels in Coconut-Cardamom Curry

Serves 4

Ingredients

2 pounds Penn Cove Mussels
2 tablespoons canola oil
2 cloves garlic, chopped
10 cardamom pods
2 cans (14-ounce) unsweetened coconut milk
½ cup dry white wine
1 tablespoon lemon juice
4 tablespoons unsalted butter, cut into pieces
Salt to taste

Directions

Rinse and scrub the mussels under cold, running water. Using your fingers or a paring knife, remove and discard the beards. In a large pot, with a tight-fitted lid, heat the oil over medium heat. Add the garlic and cardamom and cook, stirring for about 2 minutes until fragrant.

Add the coconut milk, wine and salt and simmer for 4 to 5 minutes. Add mussels and cover; increase heat to high. Cook for another 5 minutes till all mussels are open. Stir in the lemon juice and butter. Remove from heat and discard the mussels that have not opened. Serve with the broth.

Cedar-Wrapped Fresh Tilapia with Nutmeg

Serves 4

Ingredients
4 cedar grilling paper
4 tilapia fillets
2 tablespoons olive oil
Juice of 1 lemon
1 tomato, chopped
1 clove garlic, minced
½ green pepper, coarsely chopped
2 shallots, coarsely chopped
1 teaspoon chilli flakes
8 slices lime
1 tablespoon melted butter
1 teaspoon freshly grated nutmeg
Salt to taste

Directions
Soak the cedar papers in water for at least 15 minutes.

Drizzle the olive oil over the tilapia fillets, and season with salt and lemon juice. Cover and refrigerate for a minimum of 20 minutes.

In a medium mixing bowl, combine the rest of the ingredients and season with salt.

Place the cedar papers on a flat surface and place the marinated fillets over each paper. Evenly distribute all ingredients down the middle. Fold the paper and close, securing with a metal paper clip or heat-resistant band.

Preheat the oven to 350° F.

Place the filled paper on a baking sheet and bake for 12 to 15 minutes or until the fillets are cooked.

Coriander-Chilli Flakes-Crusted Red Snapper

Serves 4

Ingredients

4 (4-ounce) red snapper fillets
2 tablespoons olive oil
Juice of 1 lemon
2 tablespoons rice vinegar
4 tablespoons coriander seeds
1 tablespoon honey
2 tablespoons chilli flakes
1 teaspoon ground ginger
¼ cup chopped fresh coriander
Salt to taste

Directions

Rinse the snapper under cold water, and pat dry. In a shallow bowl, mix together the olive oil, lemon juice, rice vinegar, coriander seeds, honey, chilli flakes, ginger and salt.

Heat a non-stick skillet over medium heat. Gently rub the snapper fillets with marinade to evenly coat both sides, and place on the skillet. Cook for 2 to 3 minutes on each side until the fish flakes easily with a fork. Garnish with fresh coriander and serve hot.

Escargots with Mint-Butter Filling

Serves 4 to 6

Ingredients

8 ounces unsalted butter, softened
3 cloves garlic, minced
¼ cup minced mint leaves
1 small shallot, minced
1 teaspoon brandy
Freshly ground black pepper
24 snail shells, cleaned
24 canned escargots (giant snails)
Rock salt
8 lime wedges
Salt to taste

Directions

Beat together the butter, garlic, mint, shallots, brandy, salt and pepper in a medium-sized mixing bowl. Cover the bowl and refrigerate for at least 4 hours.

Preheat the oven to 400° F.

Divide the butter mixture into half. Using a butter knife, fill snail shells with half the mixture. Push a snail into each shell, and then use the remaining mixture to fill shells to the rim.

Cover the bottom of a baking pan with rock salt and arrange the escargots buttered-side up. Bake, for about 8 to 10 minutes until butter sizzles.

Serve hot with lime wedges.

Ginger and Sesame Seeds-Coated Wild Salmon

Serves 4

Ingredients

4 salmon fillets (6-ounce), about 1-inch thick
1 teaspoon dark sesame oil
¼ cup mixed sesame seeds
2 tablespoons finely minced fresh ginger
2 tablespoons coarsely chopped cilantro
Cooking spray
2 lemons cut into very thin slices
Salt to taste

Directions

Rinse the salmon fillets in cold water and pat dry with paper towels. Place them on a shallow glass or ceramic platter. Evenly drizzle oil over the fish and let it rest for 10 minutes.

Combine the sesame seeds, ginger, cilantro and salt in a shallow dish. Evenly dredge the fillets in sesame mixture. Spray the inside of the aluminium foil with cooking spray. Place several lemon slices on the foil and lay the fillets on top of them. Wrap each fillet, folding the edges and ends tightly. Place in a shallow pan and bake in a pre-heated oven at 425° F.

Bake for 12 to 15 minutes or until the fillets flake easily with a fork.

Lobster with Cardamom-Flavoured Clarified Butter

Serves 2

Ingredients

¼ cup clarified butter
10 cardamom pods, lightly pounded to open the pods
2 tablespoons finely chopped curly leaf parsley
1 lobster (1-pound)
1 tablespoon sea salt

Directions

Heat the clarified butter on medium heat in a saucepan. Add the cardamom pods and cook for 2 minutes. Remove from heat and add the parsley.

Place a steaming rack to hold the lobster at the bottom of a large pot. Pour 2 inches of water into the pot and add 1 tablespoon salt.

Cover the pot with the lid and bring the water to a boil. Once the water is boiling, place the lobster on the rack, cover the pot again and bring it back to a boil. Steam the lobster for 12 to 14 minutes until it is cooked. Once the lobster is done, drain the water off immediately, and serve with the cardamom-flavoured clarified butter.

Pan-Seared Orange-Saffron Salmon

Serves 2

Ingredients

2 tablespoons olive oil

2 tablespoons finely grated orange rind

1 teaspoon saffron

2 cloves garlic, minced

1 tablespoon finely chopped parsley

Freshly ground black pepper

2 (6-ounce) salmon fillets

4 slices lemon

Salt to taste

Directions

Combine the oil, orange rind, saffron, salt, garlic, parsley, and black pepper in a medium-shallow pan. Transfer the salmon fillets into the pan and gently rub with the marinade to coat evenly.

Preheat a large heavy-bottomed skillet over medium heat. Place the fillets on the skillet with the marinade. Cook for 3 minutes. Turn the fillets over, and cook for 3 to 5 minutes, or until browned and the fillets flake easily with a fork.

Transfer the fillets to individual plates, and garnish with lemon slices.

Oysters with Grapefruit Dressing

Serves 2

Ingredients

2 tablespoons freshly squeezed grapefruit juice
4 tablespoons finely chopped mint
1 (1-inch) piece fresh ginger, finely chopped
Pinch of salt
12 oysters, such as Malpeque, Kumamoto, shucked and cleaned
Crushed ice

Directions

In a small mixing bowl, combine grapefruit juice, mint, ginger and salt. Cover and refrigerate for at least an hour to blend the flavours.

Place crushed ice on a platter and top with oysters on half-shell to keep them steady. Gently spoon the grapefruit mixture on top and serve chilled.

Shrimp Sautéed with Rainbow Peppers and Pine Nuts

Serves 2

Ingredients

1 tablespoon vegetable oil

1 teaspoon minced ginger

2 cloves garlic, minced

2 cups assorted peppers, cut into 1-inch dices

4 tablespoons pine nuts

10 shrimp (size U-15; about ⅔ pound) cleaned and deveined

Freshly ground black pepper

1 teaspoon rice-wine vinegar

2 tablespoons water

1 bunch alfalfa sprouts for garnish (optional)

Salt to taste

Directions

Heat the oil over medium to high heat in a wok; add ginger and garlic and fry for a minute, stirring continuously.

Add the peppers and pine nuts and stir-fry for 3 minutes.

Toss in the shrimp, salt and pepper and cook for 2 minutes, stirring until the shrimp curls and turns opaque or pink.

Add the vinegar and water and cook for 2 minutes till all the flavours have blended. Serve hot garnished with alfalfa sprouts.

Meats & Poultry

Artichoke and Lamb Stew

Serves 2 to 4

Ingredients

6 baby artichokes
Juice of 1 lemon
2 tablespoons unsalted butter
1 (2-inch) piece cinnamon stick
2 dry bay leaves
1 pound lamb, thoroughly trimmed of fat, cut into 1 ½-inch pieces
1 medium onion, coarsely chopped
2 cloves garlic, coarsely chopped
Freshly ground black pepper
1 tablespoon all-purpose flour
1 can (28-ounce) crushed tomatoes
Salt to taste

Directions

Using a sharp paring knife, trim the outermost layer of leaves from each artichoke. Trim stems, and cut off top half of each artichoke. Place them in a medium bowl and add lemon juice, and toss to evenly coat them.

In a heavy-bottomed pot, heat the butter over high heat. Add the cinnamon, bay leaves, and lamb, and brown well on all sides.

Add onion and garlic, and season with salt and pepper. Continue to cook, stirring occasionally, for about 5 minutes until fragrant.

Add flour and stir for about 2 minutes until well combined. Add tomatoes and artichokes and pour over enough water, about 1½ to 2 cups, to just cover the meat. Reduce heat to a low, cover and simmer for about 1 hour.

Serve immediately.

Asparagus and Goat Cheese-Stuffed Beef

Serves 4

Ingredients

¼ cup goat cheese
1 tablespoon balsamic vinegar
1 clove garlic, minced
¼ teaspoon chilli flakes
Freshly ground black pepper
1 small flank steak (1 pound)
8 fresh tender asparagus
1 teaspoon olive oil
Red currants for garnish
Salt to taste

Directions

Heat broiler, with rack set 4 inches from heat. Line a rimmed baking sheet with aluminum foil; set aside.

In a medium bowl, combine cheese, vinegar, garlic, chilli flakes, salt and pepper.

Using a sharp knife, gently cut and open steak.

Cut several 12-inch pieces of kitchen twine and space evenly beneath the steak. Spread the asparagus and cheese mixture down the centre of the meat. Roll the steak over mixture, pressing firmly to compact the filling as much as possible; tie the twine to secure the roll. Cut the roll in half crosswise. Place the halves, seam-side down, on prepared baking sheet; rub with oil, and season with salt and pepper.

Broil until browned, cooking for about 8 to 10 minutes to make it medium to rare.

Let it rest, loosely covered with the foil, for 10 minutes. Remove the string, and slice the steak into 1-inch rounds and serve with red currants.

Rosemary Rubbed-
Whole Chicken

Serves 4

Ingredients

1 whole chicken (about 3 ½-pound), rinsed and patted dry inside and
   out (neck, liver, and giblets discarded)
Freshly ground black pepper
¼ cup dried rosemary
1 medium onion, quartered
2 medium carrots, peeled and cut into 1-inch dices
6 to 8 cloves garlic
Salt to taste

Directions

Preheat the oven to 475° F.

Place the chicken in a roasting pan and evenly rub with salt, pepper
and rosemary, all over.

Using the kitchen twine, securely tie the legs together; tuck the wing
tips underneath.

Stuff the cavity with the onion, carrots and garlic.

Roast in pre-heated oven for 1 to 1½ hours, or until the chicken is
cooked through and the juices run clear. Transfer to a serving platter
and let rest for about 10 minutes before serving.

Ginger-Infused Foie Gras

Serves 4 to 6

Ingredients

6 pieces of grade A foie gras (4 ounces each)
Freshly ground black pepper
¼ cup freshly squeezed ginger juice
2 tablespoons finely chopped fresh parsley
Juice of 1 lemon
1½ teaspoons unsalted butter
Salt to taste

Directions

Season the foie gras with salt and pepper.

Place a large heavy-bottomed pan over medium to high heat.

Place 3 slices in the pan and sear for about 2 minutes until golden brown. Reduce the heat slightly, turn the foie gras over, and cook for an additional 2 minutes. Transfer to a plate and set aside to rest. Wipe the pan clean and repeat with the remaining 3 slices of foie gras.

Deglaze the pan with ginger juice over medium to high heat, scraping up any browned bits with a wooden spoon. Simmer for 2 to 3 minutes or until the juice is reduced by half. Add the parsley and lemon juice and cook for another 2 minutes.

Remove from the heat and add the butter, and whisk until well combined.

Season the reduction with salt and pepper to taste. Pour it over the foie gras and serve with pineapple-celery relish (see page 102).

Honey-Cumin Spiced-Ground Turkey with Spinach

Serves 4

Ingredients

2 tablespoons vegetable oil

1 (2-inch) piece cinnamon stick

2 bay leaves

1 pound ground turkey

Freshly ground black pepper

1 large onion, finely chopped

2 cloves garlic, minced

2 Serrano chillies, seeded and minced

2 tablespoons ground cumin

1 tablespoon honey

1 tablespoon tomato paste

2 pounds fresh spinach, stems removed

Salt to taste

Directions

In a heavy-bottomed pot, heat the oil over medium heat. Add the cinnamon, bay leaves, ground turkey, salt and pepper with ½ cup water, and cook until the turkey starts to brown, stirring continuously for about 3 to 4 minutes.

Add the onion, garlic, chillies, half the cumin, honey, tomato paste, and spinach, and mix well. Cover and simmer on low heat for about 12–15 minutes, stirring occasionally.

Sprinkle with the reserved cumin and serve hot.

Garlic Crusted-Stuffed Leg of Lamb

Serves 4

Ingredients

8 cloves garlic, coarsely chopped

4 teaspoons fresh thyme leaves

4 tablespoons chopped fresh mint

Zest of 1 lemon

3 tablespoons extra virgin olive oil

1 (4-4½-pound) leg of lamb, boned and butterflied, trimmed of all
   visible fat

½ cup finely chopped pineapple

½ cup dry white wine

Salt to taste

Directions

In a small mixing bowl, combine the garlic, thyme, mint, lemon zest, and salt. Gradually add the olive oil and mix well.

Open out the lamb, skin-side down. Spread half the oil mixture over the lamb, and gently rub it. Evenly spread the pineapple with your hand.

Roll the lamb lengthwise into a uniform sausage shape about 5 inches in diameter. Tie the rolled lamb with kitchen twine at 1-inch intervals. Rub the remaining mixture over the lamb.

Wrap tightly in plastic wrap and refrigerate for at least 6 to 8 hours. Remove from the refrigerator 1 hour before roasting.

Preheat the oven to 450° F. Roast the lamb for 10 minutes. Reduce the heat to 350° and pour the wine over the lamb. Roast for 40 to 45 minutes, basting it twice while cooking with the wine.

Transfer the lamb to a carving board and allow it to rest for 15 minutes. Remove and discard the strings and cut the lamb crosswise into ½-inch-thick slices and serve.

Stuffed Quail with Apricots and Fennel

Serves 2

Ingredients

4 quails (5 ounces each)
Freshly ground black pepper
6 dried apricots, chopped
1 teaspoon fennel seeds
1 (1-inch) piece fresh ginger, minced
½ teaspoon grated orange zest
4 tablespoons pine nuts
2 tablespoons olive oil
4 tablespoons clarified butter
Salt to taste

Directions

Rinse the quails in cold water and pat it dry with paper towels. Place them on a shallow glass or ceramic platter and evenly season with salt and pepper.

In a small mixing bowl, combine the apricots, fennel, ginger, orange zest, pine nuts and olive oil. Stuff the cavity of each quail with the mixture and wrap the bird with kitchen twine to keep the stuffing in.

Preheat the oven to 300° F.

Heat the clarified butter in a heavy-bottomed skillet on medium to high heat. Gently sear the quails until evenly golden brown, about 2 minutes on each side, and place them on a roasting pan.

Roast for about 20 to 25 minutes until the quails are tender and golden brown.

Brush the quails with the melted butter twice while roasting.

Remove from the oven and serve hot with rice.

Vegetables

Allspice Infused-Carrots

Serves 4

Ingredients

2 tablespoons vegetable or canola oil

2 teaspoons allspice

1 bulb of garlic, cut horizontally

1 medium red onion, cut into 1-inch dices

1½ pounds slender baby carrots of different colours,
    trimmed, scrubbed

1 teaspoon white vinegar

1 ½ tablespoons honey

Salt to taste

Directions

Add the vegetable oil to the wok and swirl to coat the base on medium to high heat. Add the allspice and garlic, and fry until it is fragrant.

Add the onion and cook for a minute, stirring until soft.

Add the carrots, salt, vinegar and honey, and stir well.

Add ¼ cup water and reduce heat. Simmer for 3 to 4 minutes, or until the liquid has reduced, and the carrots are cooked.

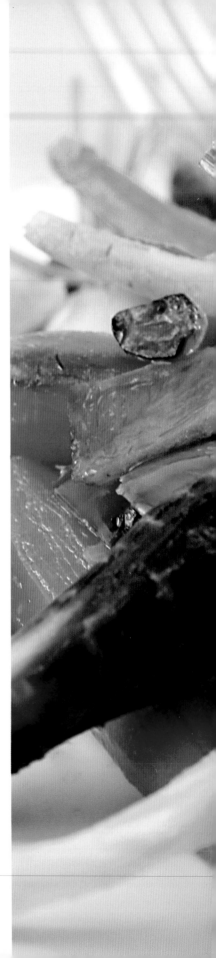

Roasted Pine Nuts with Endives

Serves 4-6

Ingredients

4 tablespoons unsalted butter
1 tablespoon vegetable oil
6 cardamom pods, lightly crushed with mortar and pestle
10 medium Belgian endives (about 3 ½ pounds), halved lengthwise
½ cup pine nuts
Freshly ground pepper
Salt to taste

Directions

Preheat the oven to 350 °F.

In a large roasting heavy-bottomed pan, heat the butter and oil on medium heat. Add the cardamom and stir continuously for 2 to 3 minutes until it is darker in colour, and very fragrant.

Remove the cardamom-infused mixture into a container.

In the same pan, arrange the endives cut-side down, in a single layer, overlapping them slightly. Scatter the cardamom mixture and pine nuts on top, and season with salt and pepper.

Roast the endives in a pre-heated oven for about 1 hour until tender turning them once or twice.

Spoon off any liquid in the roasting pan and continue to roast the endives for 15 to 20 minutes more, turning occasionally until golden and lightly caramelised.

Transfer to a platter and serve hot or at room temperature.

Stir-Fried Rainbow Swiss Chard with Roasted Garlic

Serves 4 to 6

Ingredients

2 tablespoons vegetable oil

5 cloves garlic, finely minced

1 tablespoon minced ginger

4 scallions, thinly sliced on the bias

1 tablespoon hot chilli sauce, any kind

½ teaspoon sugar

5 bunches multicolor Swiss chard, remove and tear leaves
   into 2-inch pieces

Juice of 1 lime

Salt to taste

Directions

Add the vegetable oil to the wok and swirl to coat. Add the garlic
and cook, stirring continuously until it turns golden brown and very
fragrant. Add the ginger, scallions, chilli sauce and sugar, and cook for
about 2 to 3 minutes until all the flavours are well combined.

Add the Swiss chard and season it with salt. Stirring constantly, cook
for 2 to 3 minutes until well combined. Stir in the lime juice and
serve hot.

Jalapeños Stuffed with Japanese Eggplants

Serves 6

Ingredients

2 tablespoons vegetable oil
2 cloves garlic, minced
1-inch fresh ginger root, peeled and minced
1 red onion, finely chopped
3 medium tomatoes, finely chopped
3 Japanese eggplants, finely chopped
3 tablespoons finely chopped fresh cilantro
6 large jalapeños, halved and seeded
Salt to taste

Directions

In a medium skillet heat the oil on medium to high heat.

Add the garlic, ginger, and onions, and cook stirring constantly until golden brown.

Add the tomatoes and salt, and continue to cook until the mixture becomes dry – which should take about 5 to 6 minutes. Add the eggplants and stir, cooking for 3 to 4 minutes until all the flavours are well combined. Remove from heat and transfer to a bowl.

With a small spoon, fill each jalapeño with about 1 ½ tablespoons of eggplant mixture. Place the jalapeños on a parchment or aluminium foil-lined baking sheet and bake until cooked through and bubbling, for about 10 minutes. Rotate once in the oven for even cooking.

Serve hot.

Red Potatoes with Almonds

Serves 4-6

Ingredients

3 tablespoons olive oil
2 ½ tablespoons Bengali spice mix (recipe below)
1 ½ pounds baby red potatoes, halved
2 tablespoons coarsely ground fresh Tellicherry peppercorn
¼ cup almond slivers, lightly toasted
Salt to taste

Bengali Spice mix

½ teaspoon nigella seeds
½ teaspoon black mustard seeds
½ teaspoon fenugreek seeds
½ teaspoon fennel seeds
½ teaspoon cumin seeds

Directions

Preheat the oven to 425° F.

In an oven-proof pan, heat the oil on medium heat. Add the Bengali spice mix and cook, stirring continuously for about 2 minutes until darker in colour and very fragrant.

Add the potatoes and stir to coat evenly.

On a rimmed baking sheet, evenly spread the potatoes in a single layer and season with salt and pepper. Roast for about 30 minutes, turning the potatoes once halfway through cooking, until golden brown and crisp outside and tender inside.

Toss the potatoes with almond slivers and serve hot.

Tomatillo-Squash with Saffron

Serves 4

Ingredients

½ teaspoon saffron strands
3 tablespoons unsalted butter
2 cups (about ¾ pound) small yellow patty pan squash, trimmed
6 to 8 tomatillos, hulled, washed and cut into quarters
½ teaspoon white pepper
Juice of 1 lemon
10 fresh mint leaves
Salt to taste

Directions

Soak the saffron strands in 2 tablespoons warm water and let the strands rest for 5 minutes at room temperature.

Heat the butter in a heavy-bottomed skillet on medium heat. Add the squash and tomatillos and sauté for 7 to 8 minutes, stirring occasionally until tender.

Add the saffron mixture, salt, white pepper and lemon juice, and stir well.

Transfer to a large serving dish and garnish with mint leaves.

Cinnamon-Infused Purple Cauliflower

Makes about 2 cups

Ingredients
2 tablespoons canola oil
2 (2-inch) pieces cinnamon sticks
1 teaspoon ground cumin
1 teaspoons minced ginger
2 cloves garlic, minced
1 medium purple cauliflower, cut into florets
½ teaspoon ground turmeric
1 tablespoon dried fenugreek leaves
Freshly ground black pepper
2 tablespoons chopped cilantro leaves
Salt to taste

Directions
In a heavy-bottomed skillet, heat the oil over medium heat. Add the cinnamon, cumin, ginger and garlic, and fry until the garlic begins to brown and the mixture is very fragrant.

Add the cauliflower, turmeric, fenugreek, and season with salt and pepper. Continue to cook for another 5 minutes, stirring occasionally.

Reduce the heat to low, cover the pan and cook until the cauliflower is soft. Stir occasionally. Serve hot garnished with freshly chopped cilantro leaves.

Pink Salt-Rubbed Asparagus and Sea Beans

Serves 4 to 6

Ingredients

2 teaspoons olive oil

2 tablespoons finely ground fennel seeds

¼ teaspoon pink salt

Freshly ground black pepper

1½ pounds asparagus, trimmed

½ pound sea beans

Juice of 1 lemon

Directions

Preheat the oven to 400° F.

In a small mixing bowl, combine the olive oil, ground fennel, salt, black pepper and mix until combined.

On a baking sheet, toss the asparagus and sea beans with the olive oil mixture and evenly coat the asparagus and spread in a single layer.

Transfer the asparagus to the oven and roast for 10 to 15 minutes until it is tender. Gently turn it once to ensure it is evenly cooked.

Stir in the lemon juice right before serving.

Plantains Slow-Cooked in Tamarind-Mint Curry

Serves 4

Ingredients

2 raw plantains
¼ cup tamarind paste
½ teaspoon ground turmeric
2 tablespoons vegetable oil
1 teaspoon coriander seeds
1-inch fresh ginger root, peeled and minced
2 cloves garlic, finely chopped
¼ teaspoon asafoetida
½ cup fresh mint leaves, coarsely chopped
Salt to taste

Directions

Remove the skin of the plantains, and cut into ½-inch round pieces.

In a non-reactive mixing bowl combine the plantains, tamarind pulp, salt and turmeric, and let it rest for 5 minutes at room temperature.

In a medium skillet, heat the oil on medium heat. Add the coriander seeds, ginger, garlic, asafoetida and cook for 2 to 3 minutes, stirring continuously until fragrant and the garlic turns golden brown.

Add the plantain mixture to the skillet with a cup of water. Stir well to combine all the ingredients and bring it to a boil.

Reduce the heat to low, and simmer until plantains are cooked through. Add a little more water if required.

Stir in the mint leaves and cook for another minute and serve hot.

Sides

Blackberry and Jalapeño Chutney

Makes about 1 cup

Ingredients

1 teaspoon canola oil
1 small onion, finely chopped
1 teaspoon grated fresh ginger
2 jalapeños, seeded and finely chopped
1 cup fresh blackberries
2 tablespoons red-wine vinegar
2 tablespoons brown sugar
Dash of salt

Directions

Heat the oil in a medium-sized pot on medium heat. Toss together the onions, ginger and jalapeños and fry for 3 to 4 minutes until the onions turn transparent.

Add the blackberries, vinegar, sugar, and salt and stirring frequently, cook for another 5 to 7 minutes until the liquid reduces and the flavours are well combined.

Transfer the chutney in a bowl and cool.

It can be covered and refrigerated for up to 2 weeks.

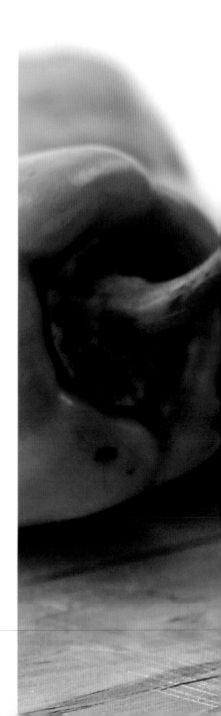

Cactus Pear, Corn Relish with Cilantro

Makes about 1 cup

Ingredients

2 ears of fresh corn, kernels removed with a knife

2 cactus pears, peeled and coarsely chopped

1 clove garlic, minced

Juice of 1 lime

1 Serrano chilli, minced

2 tablespoons chopped cilantro

Salt to taste

Directions

Mix all ingredients gently and chill for at least an hour before serving.

Pineapple-Celery Relish

Makes about 2 cups

Ingredients
1 cup fresh pineapple chunks
2 ribs of celery cut into ⅓-inch slices
¼ cup chopped onions
2 tablespoons extra virgin olive oil
2 tablespoons coarsely chopped curly leaf parsley
1 tablespoon chilli flakes
1 teaspoon finely grated fresh ginger
Salt to taste

Directions
In a large bowl, toss together the pineapple chunks, celery, onions, oil, parsley, chilli flakes, ginger, and salt. Cover and chill in the refrigerator until ready to serve.

Dates and Juniper Berries-Basmati Rice

Serves 2 to 4

Ingredients

2 cups basmati rice
12 juniper berries
1 (2-inch) long cinnamon stick
12 dates, pitted
Salt to taste

Directions

Rinse the rice in a sieve under cool running water.

Transfer to a medium pot with 3 cups of water. Add the juniper berries, salt and cinnamon, and bring to a boil. Reduce the heat to low and cook covered for about 10 to 15 minutes until the water evaporates.

Remove from heat and let stand, covered for about 10 minutes.
Use a fork to fluff the rice and gently stir in the dates, and transfer to a serving platter.

Rhubarb with Fennel Seeds and Himalayan Salt

Makes about 2 cups

Ingredients

½ red onion, finely chopped
Zest of 1 lemon
2 tablespoons fennel seeds
¼ cup white wine
2 tablespoons white-wine vinegar
½ cup packed light-brown sugar
½ teaspoon Himalayan salt
½ pound rhubarb, trimmed and cut into ½-inch pieces

Directions

In a medium saucepan, combine the onion, lemon zest, fennel seeds, wine, vinegar, sugar, and salt over medium heat and cook for about 2 minutes.

Add the rhubarb; reduce heat and continue to cook. Simmer gently for another 5 to 7 minutes until the rhubarb is tender and the mixture has thickened.

Chill until it is time to serve.

Garlic-Tomato Chutney with Mustard Seeds

Makes about 2 cups

Ingredients

2 tablespoons canola oil
4 cloves garlic, coarsely chopped
2 tablespoons black mustard seeds
1 shallot, finely chopped
4 plum tomatoes, coarsely chopped
2 tablespoons sugar
2 tablespoons rice vinegar
1 teaspoon hot sauce (optional)
Salt to taste

Directions

In a medium saucepan, heat the oil on medium heat and fry the garlic and mustard seeds for 2 minutes, stirring continuously until very fragrant and the seeds begin to sizzle. Add the shallot and cook for 3 to 4 minutes, stirring until transparent.

Add the tomatoes, sugar, vinegar, hot sauce, salt and ½ cup water and bring to a boil. Reduce the heat to simmer, cover and cook until the chutney is thick and all the flavours are blended.

Serve it warm or refrigerate up to 3 weeks.

Papaya-Shallots Salsa with Mint Leaves

Makes about 2½ cups

Ingredients

1 small ripe papaya, peeled, seeded and cut into 1-inch dices

1 medium tomato, seeded and chopped

2 shallots, finely chopped

Juice of 1 orange

¼ cup fresh mint leaves, finely chopped

1 clove garlic, minced

1 small jalapeño, seeded and chopped

Salt to taste

Directions

Combine all the ingredients in a medium mixing bowl and mix well.

Cover and refrigerate for up to 2 days.

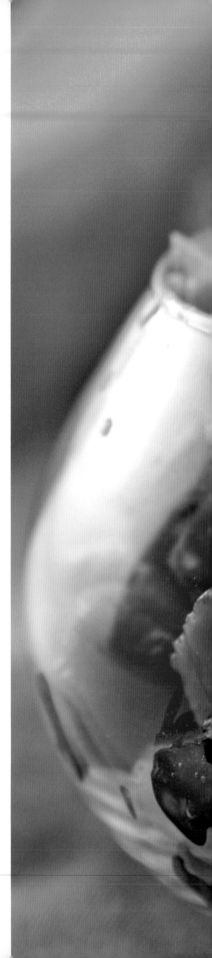

Persimmon and Pistachios with Dried Chillies

Makes about 1½ cups

Ingredients

2 tablespoons vegetable oil
4 whole dried red chillies
1 tablespoon minced fresh ginger root
½ cup pistachios, shelled
½ cup sugar
2 tablespoons lemon juice
1 teaspoon ground coriander seeds
4 soft Fuyu persimmons, peeled and cut into 1-inch cubes
Salt to taste

Directions

In a large saucepan, heat the oil over medium heat and fry the chillies for a minute. Add the ginger, pistachios, sugar, lemon juice, ground coriander seeds, salt, persimmons, and ½ cup water.

Bring to a boil and reduce the heat to simmer for 5 minutes. Cook until the persimmons are tender and the water has evaporated.

Remove from heat and let cool completely. Cover and refrigerate for up to a week.

Ginger-Raspberry Raita with Sage

Makes about 2 cups

Ingredients
1 cup plain yogurt
1 teaspoon minced fresh ginger
½ teaspoon cayenne pepper
½ pint raspberries, about 1 cup, plus a few as garnish
4 fresh sage leaves
Salt to taste

Directions
Whisk the yogurt, ginger, cayenne pepper, and salt in a bowl until the yogurt is smooth. Fold in the raspberries until just combined. Garnish with the reserved raspberries and sage leaves.

Desserts

Chocolate Roulade with Mixed-Berry Compote

Serves 10

Ingredients

10 ounces bittersweet chocolate
2 ounces unsalted butter, at room temperature
6 egg yolks and 6 egg whites
2 ounces sugar
2 teaspoons dried ancho chilli powder
¼ cup sugar
2 cups whipping cream
2 teaspoons cinnamon
Good quality cocoa powder for dusting

Directions

Preheat the oven to 350° F. Melt the chocolate and butter and allow it to cool slightly. Whisk the yolks, slowly adding the sugar and beat to ribbon stage. Sprinkle in the chilli powder. Fold yolk mixture into the cooled chocolate and set aside. Whip the whites and sugar together until soft peaks form. Fold the whites into the chocolate-yolk mixture.

Spread the mixture into a sheet pan evenly and bake for 8 to 10 minutes. Remove the roulade from the oven and cover with a damp cloth. While the roulade is cooling, whip cream with cinnamon and sugar until soft peaks form. Unmould the roulade and spread the cream evenly onto the cake, and roll to form a log. Finish by sprinkling with the cocoa powder. Serve cold.

Mixed Berry Compote

1 cup assorted fresh berries (such as raspberries, blueberries, blackberries)
3 tablespoons sugar
4 tablespoons sweet white wine such as Moscato (optional)

Combine all the ingredients.

Cover and refrigerate for at least 30 minutes before serving.

Cardamom Chai Panna Cotta with Candied Violets

Serves 6-8

Ingredients

2 teaspoons gelatin
½ cup whole milk
1½ cups heavy cream
¼ cup sugar
1 cinnamon stick
1 teaspoon ground cardamom seeds
1 tablespoon chai powder
Candied violets
Citrus short breads

Directions

Bloom the gelatin in milk.

In a medium saucepan, combine the cream, sugar, cinnamon, cardamom and chai powder and bring to a simmer. Let it stand for 5 minutes, then stir it into the gelatin mix. Strain and pour into glasses and let set overnight.

Serve cold, garnished with candied violets and citrus short breads.

Chocolate Mousse with Mixed Berries

Serves 10

Ingredients

4 large egg yolks
½ cup sugar
2 ounces bittersweet chocolate, finely chopped into even pieces
1¾ cup heavy cream
1 cup mixed berries

Directions

In a double boiler, whisk the yolks and ⅓ cup sugar for 2 to 3 minutes or until sugar has dissolved.

Turn off the heat and quickly whisk in the chopped chocolate until melted and well combined. Let it cool to room temperature.

In a medium bowl, whip the cream with the remaining sugar until soft peaks form.

Whisk half of the whipped cream into the chocolate mixture.

Layer 4 glasses with the chocolate mousse, the remaining whipped cream and berries.

Chill for at least 2 hours before serving.

Citrus Shortbread

Serves 4

Ingredients

1½ cups all-purpose flour, plus more for dusting
A pinch of salt
½ cup unsalted butter, softened
½ cup sugar
1 large egg, lightly beaten
1 lemon, peeled and rind finely chopped (about 2 teaspoons)
Juice of 1 lemon

Directions

Combine the flour, salt, butter, and sugar in a bowl. Mix with your fingers until it forms flaky crumbs. Mix in the egg, lemon rind, and lemon juice and continue to mix until the dough comes together. Form into a large ball and wrap it in plastic; refrigerate for at least an hour, preferably overnight.

Preheat the oven to 350°F.

Remove the dough from the refrigerator and let it sit for 5 to 10 minutes.

Roll the dough into ⅛ inch thickness, between two sheets of floured parchment, dusting it with flour as needed. Cut shapes with cookie cutters. Using a spatula, transfer on parchment paper on a cookie sheet.

Bake at 350°F for 8 to 12 minutes until the edges are just slightly golden brown depending on the thickness of the cookies.

Remove from the oven and let cool on a rack for 10 minutes.

Coconut Cheesecake with Nutmeg

Serves 8

Ingredients

4 cups toasted and ground cashewnuts
2 ounces melted butter
1 teaspoon cinnamon
6 ounces white chocolate
12 ounces cream cheese
½ cup sugar
A pinch of salt
1 teaspoon vanilla
2 eggs
½ cup sour cream

Directions
For Crust

Preheat the oven to 300° F.

In a food processor, add the ground cashews, melted butter and cinnamon, and pulse to combine. Divide the mixture between 3X3 sized cake rings and press until firm, and about ½-inch over the edge of the ring. Bake for about 12 to 15 minutes until set and golden. Let cool on wire rack.

Cheesecake mix

Preheat the oven to 300° F. Melt the chocolate and cool slightly.

Beat the cream cheese until very smooth, adding the sugar, salt, vanilla and chocolate until incorporated.

Add the eggs one at a time, and then add the sour cream.

Divide the cheesecake between the cake rings on top of the crumb mixture and bake for 10 to 12 minutes until set. Refrigerate until completely cool, then unmold.

Mango and Brown Egg Soufflé

Serves 6

Ingredients

2 tablespoons unsalted butter, softened
¼ cup, plus 2 teaspoons granulated sugar
½ cup mango purée
4 brown eggs, separated

Directions

Preheat the oven to 375° F

Using 1 tablespoon butter, coat the insides of 6 baking ramekins, then dust with 2 tablespoons granulated sugar.
Refrigerate until needed.

In a medium saucepan, heat the mango purée, ¼ cup sugar and remaining butter in a saucepan, and cook over medium heat for 5 minutes until sugar dissolves.

Remove from heat, cool slightly, and whisk in the egg yolks one at a time.

In a separate clean bowl, beat the egg whites just until they hold soft peaks.

Gently fold the beaten whites into the mango mixture with a metal spoon to lighten it.

Spoon the mixture into the prepared ramekins and place on a cookie sheet.

Bake on the middle rack for about 16 to 20 minutes until the soufflé is puffed and golden brown at the edges.

Serve immediately.

Ginger and Red Wine Poached Pears

Serves 6

Ingredients

Juice of 1 lemon

1 (2-inch) piece fresh ginger, peeled and coarsely chopped

1 bottle sweet red wine

2 cloves

1 (2-inch) piece cinnamon

¼ cup honey

4 cardamom seeds

1 bay leaf

6 Bartlett pears

Directions

Combine the lemon juice, ginger, red wine, cloves, cinnamon, honey, cardamom, and bay leaf in a wide medium-sized saucepan. On medium heat bring the mixture to a boil. Reduce the heat to low and simmer for another 3 to 4 minutes.

While the liquid is simmering, peel the pears, leaving the stem intact, careful not to blemish the flesh of the pears. Slice ½-inch off the bottom of the pears to create a flat bottom.

Gently place the pears in the liquid, making sure that they are in standing position and almost half dipped in the wine mixture.

Cover and continue to simmer for 8 to 10 minutes until the pears are tender and cooked through.

Remove the pears on to a serving plate. Continue to cook the sauce till the desired consistency is achieved.

Strain and serve hot with the pears.

Vanilla-Infused Plums

Serves 6

Ingredients

3 tablespoons unsalted butter
3 tablespoons sugar
1 vanilla bean, halved lengthwise, or 1 teaspoon pure vanilla extract
1 (2-inch) piece cinnamon
4 ripe plums, halved and pitted
⅓ cup apple juice

Directions

In a heavy-bottomed skillet, melt the butter over medium heat. Add the sugar, vanilla and cinnamon. Cook using a wooden spoon for two minutes, stirring until the syrup is light caramel colour.

Add the plums, tossing to coat evenly with the caramel, and cook until tender. Add the apple juice and boil until slightly thickened.

Divide the plums among 4 dessert plates and spoon the juices from the pan over each plate.

Serve hot or chilled.

Basmati Rice Pudding with Fresh Mango

Serves 4-6

Ingredients

4 cups milk

1 cup heavy cream

¾ Basmati rice, rinsed under running water

1 cup sugar

3 egg yolks

2 teaspoons vanilla extract

2 cinnamon sticks

1 ripe mango

Directions

Combine milk, cream, rice, sugar and cinnamon sticks in a heavy-bottomed pot and bring to a simmer over a low flame.

Stir occasionally and cook until rice is tender.

In a separate bowl, stir together the egg yolks and vanilla. Slowly temper into cooked rice mixture, stirring continuously until thickened.

Refrigerate until cool. Peel and dice mango into small cubes and sprinkle on top of rice pudding, and serve chilled.

Strawberry Cobbler with Almond Crust

Serves 6

Ingredients

½ cup all-purpose flour
½ cup blanched almonds, finely chopped
¼ cup packed light-brown sugar
4 tablespoons cold unsalted butter, cut into small pieces
4 cups fresh strawberries, hulled (halved or quartered if large)
2 tablespoons cornstarch

Directions

In a medium bowl, mix together flour, almonds and sugar.

Using your hands, incorporate butter into flour mixture until large, moist clumps form. Cover and refrigerate for up to one hour.

In a medium mixing bowl combine the strawberries and cornstarch and let the mixture sit for 5 minutes.

Preheat the oven to 375° F.

Divide the strawberry mixture in 6 ramekins and sprinkle evenly with chilled flour mixture.

Bake for about 45 minutes until the fruit is tender and crust is golden.

Serve hot.

Stuffed Apples with Pomegranate and Pistachios

Serves 6

Ingredients

6 large Macintosh or Empire apples
Juice of 1 lemon
¾ cup sugar
½ cup lightly toasted pistachios
¼ teaspoon ground nutmeg
½ teaspoon ground cinnamon
4 tablespoons butter, cut into pieces
¼ cup golden raisins
¼ cup dried cranberries
2 tablespoons dried pomegranate seeds, powdered or finely ground

Directions

Preheat the oven to 425°F.

Cut the top and bottom off of each apple, about ¼ to ½ inch from the stem end and reserve the tops. Gently core and hollow out each apple to make room for the filling. Sprinkle apples with lemon juice to prevent them from turning brown.

Mix the rest of the ingredients in a bowl. Overstuff the apples and replace the tops. Bake 20 minutes in a small oven-safe dish or a muffin tin to keep the apples from tumbling over.

Serve hot.

Drinks

Champagne, Blueberry and Ginger

Serves 4

Ingredients

1 (3-inch) fresh ginger root, peeled
½ cup blueberries, plus a few for garnish
3 tablespoons sugar
1 bottle (750 ml) Champagne or sparkling wine

Directions

Grate the ginger root and squeeze out the juice using a cheesecloth. Reserve the juice. Bring the ginger juice, blueberries, sugar and ¼ cup water to a boil in a small saucepan. Reduce to a simmer and cook for 15 minutes until liquid thickens.

Remove from heat and let it cool.

Purée the mixture in a blender and refrigerate for at least an hour.

Add 2 tablespoons of the mixture in each champagne glass with reserved berries for the garnish and gently pour in the champagne.

Serve chilled.

Mint-Chilli Hot Chocolate Milk

Serves 4

Ingredients

4 cups milk
3 sprigs fresh mint
1 (1-inch) piece cinnamon stick
10 ounces semisweet or milk chocolate, cut into small pieces
1 teaspoon chilli flakes

Directions

Combine milk, mint sprigs and cinnamon in a saucepan, and bring to a boil over medium to high heat. Remove from heat, and let stand for 5 to 10 minutes, covered.

Strain to remove cinnamon and mint sprigs.

Return milk to saucepan and place over medium heat. Add chocolate and whisk until chocolate is completely melted and milk is frothy.

Serve immediately sprinkled with chilli flakes.

Jasmine-Saffron Darjeeling Tea

Serves 6

Ingredients
6 cups water
4 tablespoons Darjeeling tea
1 cup fragrant dried jasmine flowers, destalked
1 teaspoon saffron strands
Sugar or honey to taste

Directions
Bring the water to a boil on high heat. Remove from heat; add the tea leaves, jasmine flowers and saffron, and cover. Let it steep for at least 15 minutes.

Serve hot with sugar or honey.

Lebanese Aphrodisiac Tea

Serves 4

Ingredients

2 star anise

4 cardamom pods

3 dried sage leaves

¼ cup dried sorrel petals

1 (2-inch) piece cinnamon stick

4 dried rose buds

½ teaspoon fennel seeds

2 teaspoons green tea leaves

Directions

Combine all the ingredients with 4 cups of water, and bring to a boil over medium heat. Reduce the heat to low, and simmer for another 2 minutes until fragrant.

Strain and serve hot.

Mango-Vanilla Cocktail

Serves 6

Ingredients

½ cup mango pulp
½ teaspoon vanilla extract
5 cups ice cubes
¾ cup tequila
Juice of 2 limes
6 fresh mint sprigs

Directions

Purée mango pulp, vanilla extract, ice, tequila, and lime juice in a blender until smooth.

Serve garnished with mint sprigs.

Peppermint-Cardamom-Liquorice Tea

Serves 6

Ingredients

2 ½ teaspoons dried liquorice root

6 to 8 cardamom pods, lightly crushed with mortar and pestle

½ cup dried peppermint leaves

2 tablespoons Darjeeling tea

½ cup honey, or to taste

Directions

Bring 6 cups of water to boil on medium to high heat. Remove from heat and add liquorice root, cardamom pods, peppermint leaves, and tea leaves; cover, and steep for 10 minutes.

Strain tea and herbs, pressing to extract all the liquid.

Stir in honey until it dissolves, and serve hot or chilled over ice.

Rose-Blood Orange Squash

Serves 4

Ingredients

2 cups water
6 drops rose essence
¾ cup sugar, or to taste
¼ teaspoon red food colouring, if desired
2 cups freshly squeezed blood-orange juice, strained
Juice of 1 lime

Directions

In a medium pot over medium heat, combine the water, rose essence, sugar, red food colouring; bring to a boil.

Remove from heat and let it cool. Add the blood-orange juice and lime juice, and chill in the refrigerator for at least 2 hours.

Serve over ice.

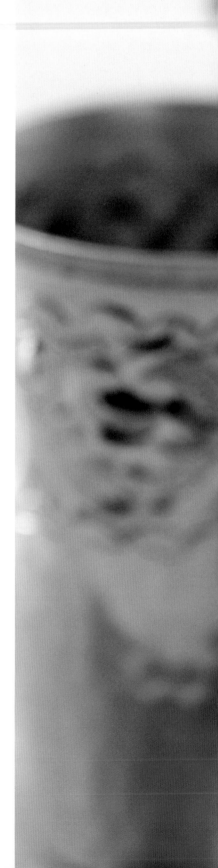

Rosebuds and Cinnamon Tea

Serves 6

Ingredients

1 (2-inch) piece cinnamon stick

3 whole cloves

24 dried rosebuds (available from online tea specialists or Indian grocery stores).

4 teaspoons honey, or to taste

Directions

Place cinnamon, cloves, rosebuds and honey in a medium pot and pour 6 cups boiling water over it and cover. Stir well and leave to stand for 2 minutes to infuse.

Strain and serve immediately.

Blossoming Tea
with Honey and Lime

Serves 4

Ingredients

4 tea blooms of your choice
2 tablespoons honey
Juice of 1 lime
1 tablespoon fresh ginger juice

Directions

Boil 4 cups of water in a medium saucepan over high heat.

Place 1 tea bloom in a heat-proof glass. Gently pour the boiling water and steep the tea bloom for 3 to 5 minutes (depending on how strong you want the tea).

Serve hot with honey, lime and ginger juice.

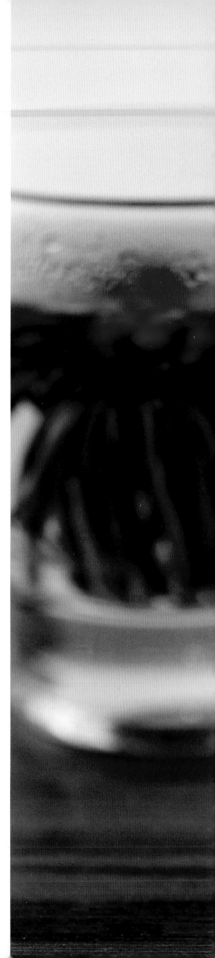

Kitchen Measurement Conversion Tables

Liquid or Volume Measures (approximate)

1 teaspoon		⅓ tablespoon	5 ml	
1 tablespoon	½ fluid ounce	3 teaspoons	15 ml	15 cc
2 tablespoons	1 fluid ounce	⅛ cup, 6 teaspoons	30 ml,	30 cc
¼ cup	2 fluid ounces	4 tablespoons	59 ml	
⅓ cup	2⅔ fluid ounces	5 tablespoons & 1 teaspoon	79 ml	
½ cup	4 fluid ounces	8 tablespoons	118 ml	
⅔ cup	5⅓ fluid ounces	10 tablespoons & 2 teaspoons	158 ml	
¾ cup	6 fluid ounces	12 tablespoons	177 ml	
⅞ cup	7 fluid ounces	14 tablespoons	207 ml	
1 cup	8 fluid ounces/ ½ pint	16 tablespoons	237 ml	
2 cups	16 fluid ounces/ 1 pint	32 tablespoons	473 ml	
4 cups	32 fluid ounces	1 quart	946 ml	
1 pint	16 fluid ounces/ 1 pint	32 tablespoons	473 ml	
2 pints	32 fluid ounces	1 quart	946 ml	0.946 litres
8 pints	1 gallon/ 128 fluid ounces	4 quarts	3785 ml	3.78 litres
4 quarts	1 gallon/128 fluid ounces	1 gallon	3785 ml	3.78 litres
1 litre	1.057 quarts		1000 ml	
1 gallon	4 quarts	128 fluid ounces	3785 ml	3.78 litres

Dry Or Weight Measurements (approximate)

1 ounce		30 grammes (28.35 g)
2 ounces		55 grammes
3 ounces		85 grammes
4 ounces	¼ pound	125 grammes
8 ounces	½ pound	240 grammes
12 ounces	¾ pound	375 grammes
16 ounces	1 pound	454 grammes
32 ounces	2 pounds	907 grammes
¼ pound	4 ounces	125 grammes
½ pound	8 ounces	240 grammes
¾ pound	12 ounces	375 grammes
1 pound	16 ounces	454 grammes
2 pounds	32 ounces	907 grammes
1 kilogramme	2.2 pounds/ 35.2 ounces	1000 grammes

Conversions
Fahrenheit to Centigrade: Subtract 32, multiply by 5, divide by 9.
Centigrade to Fahrenheit: Multiply by 9, divide by 5, add 32.

Index

Acknowledgements

Khanna Sutra: Food Lessons in Love is not a bunch of pages bound together; it's a platter of sweet memories held together by love.

As this book leaves my kitchen and celebrates its destiny in your hands, the moment would be incomplete without thinking of all the people who helped bring it to life. Some of them are directly connected to this project and love it as much as I do. We celebrated when we completed a recipe perfectly in the first go; we even celebrated the recipes that didn't work and had to be re-worked upon a few times before being presented to you.

Many thanks to my team at Juncon, our restaurant in New York, for always working dedicatedly to bring the best dining experience to the world.

Thanks also to Rajesh Bhardwaj, Andrew Blackmore and Niriti Nagpal for their unconditional support; Anirban and Rajesh for helping us with their amazing wardrobe designs used in the book; Michael Swamy, Mugdha Savkar, Mrunal Savkar and Ganesh Shedge for giving this book their all; my publisher Ajay Mago and my editor Dipa Chaudhuri for bringing this project to life, and Alpana Khare for her lovely design.

And most importantly, *Khanna Sutra* is dedicated to the indefinable emotion of love, love that has the power to move the universe.